D1090334

Date: 3/13/18

J 796.5223 FRI
Frisch-Schmoll, Joy,
Rock climbing /

PALM BEACH COUNTY
LIBRARY SYSTEM
3650 Summit Boulevard
West Palm Beach, FL 33406-4198

ROCK CLIMBING

ROCK CLIMBING

ODYSSEYS

JOY FRISCH-SCHMOLL

CREATIVE EDUCATION

Published by Creative Education
P.O. Box 227, Mankato, Minnesota 56002
Creative Education is an imprint of The Creative Company
www.thecreativecompany.us

Design by Blue Design (www.bluedes.com)
Production by Joe Kahnke
Art direction by Rita Marshall
Printed in China

Photographs by Alamy (Aurora Photos, Image Source,
lovethephoto, Natures Finest Images, Andy Teasdale, Jim
Thornburg), Creative Commons Wikimedia (Sean McCoy),
Getty Images (MIGUEL MEDINA), iStockphoto (gregepperson,
ranplett, Rumo), Mary Evans Picture Library (Grenville Collins
Postcard Collection, Mary Evans Picture Library), National
Geographic Creative (JIMMY CHIN, KEITH LADZINSKI, CORY
RICHARDS), Shutterstock (Poprotskiy Alexey, anatoliy_gleb,
lenina11only, Vitaliy Mateha, Photobac, Zeljko Radojko,
ueuaphoto)

Copyright © 2018 Creative Education
International copyright reserved in all countries. No part of
this book may be reproduced in any form without written
permission from the publisher.

Library of Congress Cataloging-in-Publication Data
Names: Frisch-Schmoll, Joy, author.
Title: Rock climbing / Joy Frisch-Schmoll.
Series: Odysseys in outdoor adventures.
Includes bibliographical references, webography, and index.
Summary: An in-depth survey of the history of rock climbing,
as well as tips and advice on how to use specific safety
equipment, and the skills and supplies necessary for different
types of climbing.
Identifiers: LCCN 2016031799 / ISBN 978-1-60818-689-1
(hardcover) / ISBN 978-1-56660-725-4 (eBook)

Subjects: LCSH: 1. Rock climbing—Juvenile literature. 2. Rock
climbing—History—Juvenile literature.
Classification: LCC GV200.2.F75 2017 / DDC 796.522/3—dc23

CCSS: RI.7.1, 2, 3, 4, 5; RI.8.1, 2, 3, 4, 5; RI.9-10.1, 2, 3, 4; RI.11-12.1,
2, 3, 4; RH.6-8.1, 2, 4, 5; RH.9-10.2, 4, 5

First Edition 9 8 7 6 5 4 3 2 1

CONTENTS

Introduction 9

From Survival to Sport 11

Making the Grade 23

Learning the Ropes 25

Climbing Tips 29

Hang On! 37

Extreme Solo Climber 39

Climbing Culture 50

A Climbing Mecca 52

Reaching New Heights 63

Ice Climbing Wonderland 69

Glossary 77

Selected Bibliography 78

Websites 79

Index 80

Introduction

Adventure awaits! It's a call from Mother Nature heard by nature lovers and thrill seekers alike. This temptation beckons them, prompting them to pack their gear, pull on their jackets, and head out the door. From mountain peaks to ocean depths and everything in between, the earth is a giant playground for those who love to explore and challenge themselves. Not content to follow the beaten

OPPOSITE: Although rock climbing can be an exciting and rewarding activity, climbers must have physical strength and a deep reserve of endurance to tackle this challenging sport.

path, they push the limits by venturing farther, faster, deeper, and higher. Going to such lengths, they discover satisfaction, excitement, and fun. Theirs is a world of thrilling outdoor adventures.

Rock climbing is one such adventure. It can take place outdoors on natural rock and cliffs or indoors on artificial, man-made walls. Climbing can take people high aboveground where only their fingertips and toes cling to the rock. Whether tackling a large boulder, participating in sport competitions, ascending a big wall over several days, or reaching a lofty mountain peak, rock climbing offers excitement in various forms. Climbers use physical strength and tools to skillfully move over vertical terrain. Offering both challenges and rewards, rock climbing is a sport with few rules but abundant opportunities for extreme adventure.

From Survival to Sport

Climbing is as old as humankind itself. For as long as people have been on Earth, we have needed to climb. For most of history, climbing was for survival. It was a basic skill and a way of life. People climbed mountains to hunt, explore, and rescue lost animals. In mountainous regions, some early peoples made their homes in steep rock cliffs where climbing was a necessity. They climbed to enter their cliff dwellings and lifted entry ladders during enemy attacks.

Sometimes climbing was a show of strength and power. To demonstrate the dominance of his kingdom to rivals, a king might order that a mountain peak be climbed. Such was the case in 1492, with King Charles VIII of France and Mont Aiguille. Antoine de Ville, a servant, led an expedition to ascend the rock tower. Using a combination of ladders, ropes, and other artificial aids, the team reached the summit, or top, as though they were storming a castle. This was the first recorded climb in history. It has been said to mark the beginning of mountaineering.

Ascending mountains, or mountaineering, combines hiking, rock climbing, and ice climbing. To train for mountain expeditions, people climbed shorter rock faces. For a long time, rock climbing was seen as only a part of mountaineering, as mountaineers would climb routes to prepare themselves for a long trek to a distant peak. Rock climbing was a way they could train to improve their overall skills.

Otherwise, for most of history, climbing mountains was done primarily out of necessity. This started to change in the middle of the 18th century with the first ascent of Mont Blanc. Mont Blanc is the highest mountain in the Alps, rising 15,781 feet (4,810 m) above sea level. The climb was the idea of Horace-Bénédict de Saussure, a Swiss nobleman and alpine traveler. After failing on his own attempt to conquer the unscaled peak, he offered a reward to anyone who could make a successful ascent. In 1786, Dr. Michel Paccard and his guide, Jacques Balmat, became the first to reach the summit. This famous climb is often considered the beginning of rock climbing.

The sport of rock climbing began to develop in the late 1800s in European countries such as Great Britain, Germany, and Italy. It was looked upon as a sport in England in 1886 after the first free solo ascent of the

Napes Needle by Walter Parry Haskett Smith. Regarded as the "father of rock climbing," Haskett Smith climbed the 70-foot (21 m) pinnacle wearing nailed boots and without the aid of ropes, hammering spikes, or ladders. This solo climb was the earliest recorded rock climb done purely for enjoyment, and it was widely publicized. Newspapers printed photos of Haskett Smith atop the pointed spire. As the recreational pastime caught on, more people started to explore other peaks and mountain ranges around the world.

In Germany, the sport of climbing got a boost from Rudolf Fehrmann and American Oliver Perry-Smith. As a team, they pushed the limits of risk and difficulty on steep sandstone spires near Dresden, making many first ascents. In 1887, a teenager named Georg Winkler became well-known for his solo climbs in the Dolomites,

With better equipment, people started conquering climbs that had not been attainable before.

a mountain range in northeastern Italy. His success encouraged acceptance and development of the sport in that area.

As the century went on and more people wanted to climb, equipment improved. Special climbing ropes and other gear were introduced in the early 1900s. With better equipment, people started conquering climbs that had not been attainable before. By the 1920s, rock climbing was known in the United States as an essential part of mountain climbing. During the 1950s, it became its own sport.

As the years passed, the trend became to make shorter but more difficult climbs. Rather than trek to a distant peak on an expedition, climbers shifted their focus to

In September 1905, Rudolf Fehrmann and Oliver Perry-Smith were the first to reach the summit of the Barbarine, a rock formation in the Elbe Sandstone Mountains, which straddle the southeastern German border with part of the Czech Republic.

technically tough climbs. Safety measures and protective gear were developed as the routes became harder and riskier. The history of rock climbing is similar to that of mountaineering, in the sense that climbers were eager to try increasingly difficult routes. They were determined to climb steeper cliffs and outdo one another. As a result, different climbing styles emerged based on the terrain and the use of ropes and other gear.

Grading systems were developed to compare the difficulty level of climbs. Because rock climbing became known to various countries at different times, many countries made their own grading system. A route is given its grade by the first person to climb it. For that reason, grades should be viewed as general guides, since no two climbers think exactly alike. The Yosemite Decimal System (YDS)—called the Sierra Club grading system

in the 1930s—classified hikes and climbs in the Sierra Nevada, a major mountain range in California. It is the system still used in the U.S. today. It covers a range from 1 to 5. Great Britain, Australia, South Africa, Germany, and France each have their own grading systems.

Climbing techniques as well as gear and equipment have improved to help advance the sport of rock climbing. This has enabled climbers to tackle even more extreme walls and take on greater challenges. Today, climbing comes in many different types, styles, and variations. It can be traditional climbing, sport climbing, bouldering, ice climbing, or part of mountaineering. Each type is a distinct discipline that demands specialized skills. In the 1980s, rock climbing also moved indoors to man-made rock walls in gyms and clubs.

Rock climbing offers great variety to both newcomers and experts who have dedicated themselves to the sport. Although it is a risky activity that requires physical strength and endurance, it offers an exciting challenge. The adrenaline rush it provides is probably one of the reasons so many people are so passionate about it. Following in the footsteps of the climbing pioneers and blazing their own routes, a new generation of super climbers is taking the sport to new heights.

Making the Grade

Climbers have developed rating systems so they know how hard a climb will be. In the U.S. and Canada, the most widespread rating system is called the Yosemite Decimal System.

There are five classes:

Class 1:   Walking on flat ground.

Class 2:   Hiking on an uneven trail.

Class 3:   **Scrambling** on rocks steep enough that you may have to use your hands but not rope.

Class 4:   Climbing that is hard to do without some support from a rope.

Class 5:   Rock climbing that needs gear for safety. Unroped falls can result in severe injury or death. Routes are further graded on a scale from 5.1 to 5.15 to indicate difficulty.

For bouldering, ratings are based on the V-Scale, which ranges from V0 to V16.

Learning the Ropes

The technical challenges of rock climbing vary greatly, depending on the terrain and type of climbing. As the degree of difficulty increases, so typically does the need for more specialized equipment. As a general rule, the higher and more difficult the climb, the more gear it requires. Climbers must have the appropriate gear if they become serious about the sport.

Some basic equipment is needed to

OPPOSITE: Sporting proper safety equipment, such as helmets and harnesses, greatly improves a climber's chances of reaching the summit without injury.

begin climbing. To improve one's grip and footing on a climbing wall or rock face, special footwear is usually worn. Designed with a sticky rubber layer, the thin, snug-fitting shoes allow the climber to "feel" the rock more easily. A climbing helmet is also worn to protect a climber's skull against falling debris such as rocks and from any impact during a fall. Clothing needs to be comfortable and suited for the conditions and temperature. It should allow climbers to move freely without restricting their movements. Form-fitting clothing is best because it allows climbers an unobstructed view when looking for secure footholds.

A safety harness is another primary piece of equipment. It is used for connecting a rope to the climber and protecting climbers if they fall. Harnesses are worn around the hips and have loops where climbers can attach

BELOW Metal clips, called carabiners, come in many shapes, weights, and sizes. Climbers use them for everything from carrying equipment on their belts to securing ropes to rocks.

Climbing Tips

Successful climbing requires a plan. Look around and decide where you will move your hands and feet. Think ahead to your next moves. Look all around for handholds and footholds, not just up. There might be good options on either side of you. Be smooth and steady, and take short steps. Move only one limb at a time. By keeping your hands around shoulder height, you'll be better able to balance. Overreaching will also strain and tire your arms. Handholds should be used for balance only, not pulling up. Push down on your footholds and straighten your legs to move upward. Your leg muscles are much stronger than your arm and shoulder muscles. By relying on them, you can climb longer and higher.

their gear. There are two loops at the front of a harness where the climber ties the rope using a figure-eight knot. A harness should not be too loose or it may slip off. A belaying device, which helps control a climber when he is rappelling, is sometimes attached to the harness. Chalk bags are also found on the harness. They are widely used as a way of drying sweaty hands and preventing slippage.

Specially designed ropes are used for climbing. They consist of an inner core of long twisted fibers and an outer layer of woven colored fibers. Climbing ropes can be divided into two classes: dynamic and static. Dynamic ropes have some "give," which means that they can stretch a bit. They are meant to absorb some of the impact of a falling climber and therefore offer some protection. They are usually used as belaying ropes. Static ropes are less flexible and are used for anchoring and rappelling.

Carabiners, or "biners" as they are commonly known, are D-shaped metal loops used as connectors in climbing. With spring-loaded gates, the lightweight but strong biners come in a variety of forms, according to their use. Locking carabiners provide additional security to climbers, since the gate can be locked while in use. They are used for important connections such as belaying devices and in anchoring. Two non-locking biners can be connected by a short length of nylon webbing to create a quickdraw.

Climbers rely on quickdraws, or runners, to connect ropes to bolt anchors or to other traditional protection. They allow a rope to move through the anchoring system with minimal friction. Quickdraws are also frequently used in indoor climbing, where they are pre-attached to the wall. When a climber ascends, she clips the rope through the runner in order to secure herself to the wall and thereby minimize the distance if she falls.

Belaying devices are a type of braking system used to control a rope when belaying. The main purpose is to

OPPOSITE On steep ascents, some climbers insert anchors into the rocks to prevent themselves from falling long distances if they happen to lose their grip.

allow the rope to be stopped and locked off with minimal effort. This should stop a climber's fall. Multiple kinds of belaying devices exist, some of which are used for controlled descents on a rope, as in rappelling. Some devices rely on the belayer's brake hand and a carabiner to lock off the rope. Others have a built-in mechanism that locks off the rope automatically without the help of any other pieces of equipment.

In traditional rock climbing, there is a lot of special equipment and hardware. Together, these devices are called protection. They provide a way to place temporary anchor points on a rock. A wide range of protection is used to safeguard a climber against the consequences of a fall. Typical hardware includes nuts, hexes, and cams. Nuts are small blocks of metal attached to a loop of cord or wire. They come in different shapes and sizes.

Their sides can be straight or curved. Climbers wedge them into narrow cracks in the rock and then give a tug to set them. Similar to nuts, hexes are hollow six-sided shapes with tapered ends. They are threaded with cord or webbing. Climbers jam these metal pieces into cracks and set them so that they won't pull out.

Cams are another tool climbers insert into crevices as protection. Sometimes known as spring-loaded camming devices, cams have an axle with expanding parts. When wedged into a crack, the springs expand and grip the rock face. The harder a climber pulls on a cam, the more it resists being pulled out. A climbing rope can then be attached to the end of a cam's stem using a sling—a loop of nylon tape or rope—and a carabiner. It takes a lot of practice to learn to set nuts and cams, and to recognize where and how they will fit in the rock. As a climber uses his gear and sets the protection in the rock, he also searches for handholds and footholds to ascend. Climbers use a combination of special moves, grips, and techniques to move up a rock wall. A variety of knots is needed in rock climbing, so knowing how to tie a proper knot is essential for climbers.

Climbing can be enjoyed in locations all around the world, in very different environments, from deserts to icy regions. Most climbers choose to climb during warmer months of the year because being cold with numb fingers and toes makes it hard to hold on to a rocky surface. But there are some extreme climbers who choose to climb ice in cold regions during the winter. In addition to warm clothing, this type of climbing requires special equipment such as crampons and ice tools.

Hang On!

As an extreme sport, rock climbing has high levels of difficulty and intensity. Despite the risks and dangers involved, participants often find themselves tempted by great heights and imposing walls. The element of danger is what draws some enthusiasts to this adventurous activity. As sports become more extreme, they become more dangerous. The cliffs get higher and the protection decreases. Extreme

OPPOSITE: Not only does rock climbing take strength and flexibility, but it also requires mental toughness and the ability to find the best next step, reach, or fingerhold.

athletes are exposed to riskier situations. Mistakes and accidents can easily occur, even to the experts. Sadly, climbing has claimed many lives.

All climbers should be familiar with the potential hazards and work to minimize the risks. Ropes and equipment should be inspected before every climb. No matter one's skill level, all climbers should climb within their abilities and avoid difficult routes that are beyond their limits. Beginners can sign up for a week-end class or get one-on-one instruction from a certified

Extreme Solo Climber

Climbing without a rope represents the ultimate extreme in rock climbing. Alex Honnold is an American climber best known for his free solo ascents of big walls, the riskiest kind of climbing. In February 2014, he scaled an extremely dangerous route in Mexico with no safety gear. Using nothing but his bare hands, climbing shoes, and a bag of chalk dust, he ascended the 2,500-foot (762 m) cliff face. The climb is believed to be one of the world's most difficult, rated 5.12 on the YDS. Most climbers take two days to complete the climb with ropes and assorted safety gear, but Honnold finished it in just three hours, hanging on with his toes and using his fingertips to grip the tiny crevices along the route.

Indoor rock walls offer both beginners and advanced climbers the thrill of the climb without the added strain of having to deal with other factors, such as changeable weather.

When starting out, it is best to learn the essentials from an experienced climber and to do a lot of easy climbs.

climbing guide. When starting out, it is best to learn the essentials from an experienced climber and to do a lot of easy climbs. Children should always climb with an adult who will supervise the climbing session. Knowledgeable instructors can teach beginners about correct form and technique. This will keep them from developing unsafe habits. The proper use of harnesses, helmets, and other safety gear, plus the observance of safety precautions, will go a long way in keeping a climber safe.

Out in the natural environment, many factors can affect a climber's well-being. Temperatures can quickly drop, and sudden changes in weather or instances of injury can strand a climber on a cliff for a while before rescue is possible. Loose rock and falling debris are other potential hazards. In locations of high altitude, the possibility of an avalanche is an additional hazard for those seeking to climb mountain peaks. Wherever they choose to climb, climbers should become familiar with the particular environment and be prepared for any adversity that may come their way.

Knowing the risks is an important aspect of climbing, but that is only part of the equation. The other part is responding to those risks and taking the necessary pre-

cautions to ensure a safe and fun climbing experience. Climbing can be a safe activity given proper equipment, expert instruction, and the dedicated use of safety techniques. Properly caring for and using the correct ropes and other gear should be a habit.

Another aspect of climbing is mental toughness. The fear of falling is a natural instinct. Hanging by one's fingertips on the side of a rock wall can be exhausting and stressful. Quite often, a person's attempts at climbing will end in failure as he falls and dangles on the rope. Climbing is a process, and to succeed, participants must embrace and learn from those failures. Falling is part of the sport, but climbers can learn how to reduce their chances of injury. To improve, they must keep working to figure out the climb and approach the challenge.

Experts with advanced skills can take greater chances

by attempting extreme climbs. Will Gadd from Canada is one of those extreme athletes. An accomplished traditional, sport, and competition climber, Gadd is also one of the world's best ice climbers. In January 2015, he made a historic climb up one of the world's most famous waterfalls, Niagara Falls. This natural wonder straddles the border of Canada and the U.S. While plenty of people have gone down Niagara over the years, Gadd became the first person to ever go *up* the falls. Thanks to a cold winter, the falls became frozen enough to climb. To aid in his record-setting ascent, Gadd used ice axes, crampons, and an ice hook.

Also in January 2015, Tommy Caldwell and Kevin Jorgeson achieved one of climbing's most difficult challenges. Over the course of 19 days, they reached the summit of the Dawn Wall section of El Capitan in California. In doing so, they became the first to ever free climb the entire length of this extremely difficult route. They used their hands and feet to ascend the rock, employing ropes and other gear only to stop a fall. Approximately 3,000 feet (914 m) tall, the Dawn Wall involves 32 pitches—in terms of rope lengths—of climbing. To avoid the daytime heat, they did much of their climbing at night, aided by headlamps. They slept 1,500 feet (457 m) above the valley in a portaledge, which is a hanging tent designed for climbers who spend multiple days and nights on a big wall.

Historically, rock climbing has encountered its share of controversies. The topic of artificial aids is one that attracts debate. Some people have argued strongly against it and about what items can or should be used. They claim that true climbers do not rely on aids. Other climbers have been in favor, stating that artificial aids allow ascents of otherwise unclimbable walls. The use of chalk has been another area of conflict. Some climbers use it to place "tick marks" to help them locate handholds and footholds that would otherwise be hard to see. While chalk allows for more secure handholds, some think the remaining residue on the rock is an eyesore.

Drilling bolts leaves a more permanent mark. Those in favor believe it makes climbing safer. Yet the other side of the issue points to the environmental damage to

OPPOSITE Aids such as chalk marks and permanent bolts can add safety to the route, but they take away climbers' freedom to scale their own paths to the top.

the natural rock. Installing protection bolts is needed in some areas to climb sections of rock that have no cracks, which is where climbers typically find handholds and footholds and place their climbing protection. To minimize the impact to the environment and care for the rock, climbers should not add bolts where they do not already exist. Removable gear has less impact on the rock because it does not cause permanent damage to the rock surface. Being a responsible climber involves showing respect by not disturbing or removing vegetation along a climb. Climbing is at its best when climbers can challenge and enjoy themselves safely and without harming the environment.

Climbing Culture

Climbing is divided into several distinct styles and categories, with each one using its own particular techniques, equipment, and environments. Rock climbing itself is divided into three separate disciplines: traditional climbing, sport climbing, and bouldering.

Traditional climbing is the original style of climbing. A lead climber places removable gear such as cams and nuts for protection as he climbs. This protects him and his climbing partner from falling off a cliff. Most traditional climbs follow cracks where the lead climber can easily wedge in his gear. To climb most multi-pitch routes, a climber needs to have traditional skills. This type of climbing offers extreme adventure up high on cliffs and on big walls. Climbers must ascend long routes, figuring out where and how to go as they climb. They blaze their own path up the rock. Multi-day climbs require that climbers carry supplies such as food and shelter. This kind of climbing is also known as big-wall climbing. A lot of specialized gear is needed for big-wall climbing to secure climbers to the rock.

In sport climbing, climbers don't have to carry as much gear. They are protected with preplaced bolts that are left in the rock. This type of climbing involves ascending cliffs

A Climbing Mecca

El Capitan is a rock formation in California's Yosemite National Park. It is located on the north side of Yosemite Valley and is part of the Sierra Nevada mountain range. El Capitan's 2,916 vertical feet (889 m) of granite was once considered impossible to climb, but now it's the standard for big-wall climbing. It is one of the world's greatest challenges for climbers. As many as 60 climbers may dot El Capitan on a good day. There are numerous routes, but the most popular and famous is the Nose. This route was first climbed in 1957–58 by Warren Harding, Wayne Merry, Rich Calderwood, and George Whitmore. They climbed the Nose in 47 days over a span of 17 months. Today, expert climbers can ascend it in a few hours.

usually less than 100 feet (30.5 m) high. The emphasis is on pushing one's limits, trying hard routes, and doing gymnastic-like moves. Enthusiasts of sport climbing can show off their athletic movements and pursue difficult routes in a relatively safe environment, thanks to the permanent bolts and anchors that offer protection. Bolts are installed in holes drilled in rock, which permanently alters the rock surface. Sport climbing is much safer than traditional climbing, but there is less freedom because the climbers don't get to choose their own routes. They have to follow the trail of bolts. Areas for sport climbing are found everywhere in the U.S. and Canada.

The third discipline of rock climbing takes place closer to the ground. But that doesn't mean it is any easier. Bouldering involves climbing on blocks of rock or small faces up to 20 feet (6.1 m) high. The route or sequence

OPPOSITE Bouldering involves navigating a section of rock that is low to the ground; therefore, this activity requires much less equipment than other types of climbing.

of climbing is called a problem. The goal in bouldering is to ascend a problem without a rope, harness, or gear. Bouldering requires only rock shoes, chalk, and a crash pad made of thick foam to cushion landings. It is often a social type of climbing where people take turns spotting one another in the landing zone. The low height means that climbers are usually within jumping distance of the ground, but spotters are there, anyway. They help direct a fall and prevent injury. Bouldering is good training for other types of climbing. It makes a person stronger and enables him to practice a variety of climbing moves just aboveground. Bouldering is considered a pure form of climbing, since it does not require ropes or complicated gear.

The small town of Bishop, California, is surrounded by some of the country's best bouldering spots, with di-

For novices, top-rope climbing is the best introduction to the sport of climbing.

verse boulders and interesting problems. At this location and others around the world, bouldering is a popular activity that has evolved into a sport of its own. There are clear advantages to bouldering. It offers a good way to practice footwork, develop balance, and experiment with different ways of moving on a vertical space. Since climbers rarely climb more than several feet off the ground, it's easy and safe to jump off and try something different. A person can pick a problem and focus on solving it, even if that means stopping mid-climb to start over repeatedly.

For novices, top-rope climbing is the best introduction to the sport of climbing. It is the most popular option for beginners and the safest way to climb, since falls are short. It involves ascending cliffs or indoor walls with the safety rope always anchored above the climber. With that anchor in place, a climber is never at risk when taking a fall. Top ropes provide a more controlled environment than lead climbing, where improperly placed or faulty gear may pull out. Top-roping requires only basic climbing equipment, and climbing areas are found anywhere there are cliffs. It is an excellent way to practice and develop skills. With top-roping, it's a belayer, not a spotter, who keeps watch to protect a climber. One end of the rope is attached to the climber, and then the rope goes through an anchor at the top. The opposite end is attached to the belayer, who stops the rope if the climber falls.

Another type of climbing is aid climbing, where a climber ascends by using climbing equipment to support his weight. A climber places protection in order to stand on it or pull himself up to make upward progress. Climbers might use hook-and-ladder like devices, called aiders or stirrups, which are attached to other gear to support the climber's weight. In general, aid climbing is done on routes where free climbing with just hands and feet is difficult or impossible. It is used on extremely steep and long routes that require great endurance as well as physical and mental stamina.

Aid climbing takes a back seat to free climbing, which is the mainstream style of climbing today. In free climbing, no aids are applied, and gear is used only to prevent a climber from falling. Free climbing is much

BELOW Deep-water soloing is a form of solo rock climbing practiced on sea cliffs. Climbers rely on water below them to "catch" them if they fall.

more athletic than aid climbing. Free climbing does not mean climbing with no rope. That is free soloing, a supremely risky style of climbing performed by only a handful of experts.

Mountaineering, or alpinism, combines different kinds of climbing. Alpinists encounter and must know how to travel over rock, cliffs, snow, and ice. A thorough knowledge of rock, aid, ice, snow, and mixed climbing is essential. Scaling mountain peaks requires advanced experience, so mountaineers are some of the best climbers in the world. These experts are well-rounded in their abilities and possess an extensive range of climbing skills.

Mountaineers are experts who have the skills and experience to handle all types of climbing conditions, from sheer cliffs to ice and snow.

Reaching New Heights

Most people begin climbing for the rush of the new experience and the thrill of the challenge. Before long, the motion of climbing and the feeling they get from it hooks them. They discover that climbing can be exciting, no matter their age or ability level. Children as well as adults can learn to climb and benefit from it. It is a fun sport that offers both physical and mental health benefits. Being outdoors

OPPOSITE: Rock climbing improves physical fitness, boosts problem-solving skills, and rewards climbers with a feeling of accomplishment.

provides the chance to enjoy nature as well. Some climbers aspire to climb for fun or to become physically fit. Others want to advance their skills so that they can attempt more difficult crags.

Climbing offers many challenges and rewards that are different from other sports. It engages both the mind and body and is never boring. Each climb offers the opportunity for improvement. Like doing a puzzle, a climber uses problem-solving skills to figure out the sequence of moves needed to complete a route. It is a sport that challenges a person's flexibility, stamina, and almost every muscle in the body. In addition to getting physically stronger, people climb to stretch their personal limits and gain a sense of accomplishment after scaling a difficult wall. Climbing is about overcoming obstacles, and climbers love a good challenge.

Some enthusiasts love climbing for the opportunities to compete. Top performers participate in competitions around the world, from U.S. national championships to the World Cup. In the U.S., USA Climbing (USAC) is the governing body of competition climbing. Competitions range from local events for all ages and abilities to pro and World Cup events. Such high-level events grow bigger every year and include bouldering, sport climbing, and speed climbing. Joining USA Climbing gives climbers the chance to put their skills to the test by participating in organized competitions. Participants are grouped into divisions by age.

The International Climbing and Mountaineering Federation (UIAA) was developed in France in 1932. Since then, it has promoted safe climbing, helped to

OPPOSITE Competitive sport climbing has gained a toehold in the Olympics, where it will be an official event in the 2020 Games in Tokyo.

preserve mountain environments, and hosted some of the largest climbing competitions in the world.

For competitive climbing, the International Federation of Sport Climbing (IFSC) is the governing body. The IFSC World Cup is a series of climbing competitions in which athletes compete in three disciplines: lead climbing, bouldering, and speed climbing. In technical climbing competitions, climbers must sometimes climb the route *on sight*, which means they are not allowed to see the route beforehand or get advice from other climbers. They have only a limited amount of time to inspect the route before they compete.

Across North America, there are also several ice climbing competitions and festivals. These events can last for several days and include the best competitors from around the world. Ice climbing was presented as

Ice Climbing Wonderland

The Ouray Ice Festival is the largest ice climbing festival in North America. Each January, the world's top ice climbers, gear manufacturers, and ice climbing enthusiasts come to southern Colorado to celebrate and challenge themselves. Professional climbers power their way up the latest competition routes in both mixed climbing and speed climbing competitions. For months beforehand, ice farmers carefully create the massive slabs and pillars of ice. Using 7,500 feet (2,286 m) of irrigation pipes and 235 shower heads, they create more than 200 ice climbing routes. The Ouray Ice Park is a famous destination for climbers of all abilities and a celebration of ice climbing. In operation for more than 20 years, the man-made park is free and has a special climbing area for kids.

a cultural event at the 2014 Winter Olympics for the first time in Sochi, Russia. It may become an Olympic event in the future.

Climbing is a physically taxing sport that requires a lot of body control and strength. Climbers train to meet the rigorous demands in a number of ways. To build stamina and endurance, many climbers cycle, run, ski, and hike in addition to climbing. To build strength, they lift weights and do pushups, pull-ups, and sit-ups. They also use special equipment such as hangboards and campus boards to improve arm and finger strength. The muscles in the fingers, hands, and forearms are perhaps the most important for climbing. If those muscles are weak, a climber won't make it up many routes.

Rock climbing is a total-body workout, so having a powerful upper body, lower body, and core will prepare a climber for long routes and difficult moves. Before training or starting to climb, climbers should always warm up by stretching all their muscles. Flexibility is important because climbing involves reaching, stretching, and being in awkward positions. To help them train more effectively, climbers should eat a healthy diet, stay hydrated, and get plenty of rest.

Climbing is a mental challenge as well. Steep cliffs and big walls expose climbers to incredible danger and stress. They must face such situations with intense focus, willpower, and perseverance. Being alert, aware, and relaxed is essential in climbing. The fear of heights and fear of falling are natural instincts, but climbers learn to manage these fears by thinking clearly and making good decisions regarding risks and safety.

Climbing is one of the fastest-growing sports today and getting involved is fairly easy. Many people get started by going to an indoor climbing gym. In areas where natural rock climbing isn't available or when the weather is too wet or cold, an indoor climbing wall is a great alternative. In a gym, a climber can practice year round. Most major cities have at least one climbing gym with colorful, multifaceted walls, cushioned floors, and bouldering crash pads. Beginners can rent all the climbing equipment they need.

Most gyms offer customized classes to suit each person's ability, where newcomers can get instruction on proper technique and learn safety skills. Experienced climbers can use the gym to try out new techniques and specialized moves. Indoor climbing still has risks, but they are minimized because the climbing occurs in a controlled environment where safety measures are in place. Climbing clubs are another great way to get introduced to the sport. They offer courses and guided climbing trips where beginners can get hands-on instruction from experienced climbers.

Built on the site of a former quarry, the Edinburgh International Climbing Arena in Scotland is one of the largest indoor climbing facilities in the world.

Getting vertical in rock climbing is an ultimate adventure and thrill. On soaring granite walls, large boulders, and rock surfaces of all kinds, this extreme sport lives up to the expectations of any climbing enthusiast. Every ascent is a chance to learn something new and come away with a sense of accomplishment. The lessons learned on the rock can be applied to other parts of one's life. In the great outdoors—and indoors at a gym wall—rock climbing is an exhilarating and rewarding experience. For many people, it is more than just a sport. It's a passion and a way of life.

Glossary

adrenaline	a hormone produced by the adrenal glands to aid the body in meeting physical or emotional stress, characterized by increased blood flow and heightened excitement
artificial aids	devices used by climbers to progress upward and to climb blank walls that do not have features such as cracks and crevices
belaying device	a metal piece attached to a harness that is used to hold a climber; the rope runs through the device, using friction to hold the climber if he falls
big wall	a tall cliff that usually requires more than a single day for a climber to summit
campus boards	training tools used to improve finger strength and rock climbing performance; a person ascends or descends a series of thin slats using only her hands
crags	steep, rugged masses of rock projecting upward or outward
crampons	metal plates with spikes attached to footwear for snow walking, mountaineering, and ice climbing
friction	the action of one surface or object rubbing against another

multi-pitch	describing a climb that is broken into a series of several pitches, because the climb is too high to be done in one standard rope length
rappelling	descending a cliff face or rock wall while suspended from a rope
scrambling	making one's way up a steep slope or over rough ground by using the hands and feet

Selected Bibliography

Creasey, Malcolm, Neil Gresham, and Nigel Shepherd. *Rock Climbing: A Practical Guide to Essential Skills*. London: Southwater, 2007.

Gaines, Bob. *Toproping*. Guilford, Conn.: FalconGuides, 2012.

Green, Stewart M., and Ian Spencer-Green. *Rock Climbing, a Beginner's Guide: From the Gym to the Rocks*. Guilford, Conn.: Knack, 2010.

Hill, Pete. *The Complete Guide to Climbing and Mountaineering*. Cincinnati: David and Charles, 2008.

Horst, Eric J. *Learning to Climb Indoors*. 2nd ed. Guilford, Conn.: FalconGuides, 2012.

Long, Steve. *The Climbing Handbook: The Complete Guide to Safe and Exciting Rock Climbing*. Richmond Hill, Ont.: Firefly Books, 2007.

Van Tilburg, Christopher. *The Adrenaline Junkie Bucket List: 100 Extreme Outdoor Adventures to Do before You Die.* New York: St. Martin's Press, 2013.

Websites

Grog's Climbing Knots
http://www.animatedknots.com/indexclimbing.php#ScrollPoint

This website describes various knots used for climbing and gives step-by-step animated directions.

Kidz World: Rock Climbing Gear
http://www.kidzworld.com/article/3668-rock-climbing-gear

This website gives kid-friendly information on the gear needed for rock climbing and contains links to other climbing-related information.

Note: Every effort has been made to ensure that any websites listed above were active at the time of publication. However, because of the nature of the Internet, it is impossible to guarantee that these sites will remain active indefinitely or that their contents will not be altered.

Index

bouldering 21, 23, 50, 53, 55–56, 65, 67, 72
Caldwell, Tommy 45
    and Jorgeson, Kevin 45
competitions 10, 45, 65, 67, 69
    IFSC World Cup 65, 67
    Olympics 69
    Ouray Ice Festival 69
conservation 47, 49, 67
dangers 18, 21, 33, 37–38, 41–42, 44, 51, 55, 60, 70–71, 72
El Capitan 45–46, 52
    and the Dawn Wall 45–46
equipment 12, 15, 16, 18, 20, 23, 25–26, 29–31, 33–35, 38, 39, 41, 44–47, 49–51, 53, 55, 57–58, 60, 69, 72
    belaying devices 29, 30, 31, 33
    carabiners 30, 33, 34
    chalk 29, 39, 47, 55
    crampons 35, 45
    footwear 15, 26, 39, 55
    hardware 33–34, 50
    harnesses 26, 29, 41, 55
    helmets 26, 41
    ropes 12, 15, 16, 18, 23, 26, 29–30, 31, 33, 34, 38, 39, 44, 46, 55, 57–58, 60
Fehrmann, Rudolf 15
    and Perry-Smith, Oliver 15
Gadd, Will 45
    and Niagara Falls 45
grading systems 18, 20, 23, 39
    Yosemite Decimal System (YDS, or Sierra Club grading system) 18, 20, 23, 39
Harding, Warren 52
    and team members 52
Haskett Smith, Walter Parry 15
Honnold, Alex 39
ice climbing 13, 21, 35, 45, 60, 67, 69
indoor climbing walls 10, 21, 31, 57, 71–72, 76
Mont Aiguille 12

and King Charles VIII 12
Mont Blanc 13–14
mountaineering 13, 18, 21, 60, 65
Napes Needle 15
organizations and clubs 21, 65, 67, 72
    International Climbing and Mountaineering Federation (UIAA) 65, 67
    International Federation of Sport Climbing (IFSC) 67
    USA Climbing (USAC) 65
Paccard, Dr. Michel 14
    and Balmat, Jacques 14
Saussure, Horace-Bénédict de 13–14
Sierra Nevada 20, 52
weather 26, 35, 41, 46, 71
Winkler, Georg 15–16
Yosemite National Park 52